We Live in Australia

Donna Bailey and Jean Chapman

MACMILLAN

Hello! My name is Ken.

I live in Sydney.

Sydney is the biggest city in Australia.

It is built around a natural harbour

which has a lot of bays and inlets.

Our house is in North Sydney on
the north shore of Sydney Harbour.
To drive to the business centre of Sydney
we must cross over Sydney Harbour Bridge.

When Dad goes to work, he goes across
Sydney Harbour by ferry.
There are ships, sailing boats and
ferries in the harbour.

Ships come to Sydney from
all over the world.
The docks are always very busy with
big ships and small ships loading and
unloading their cargoes.

Many people who live in Sydney spend
a lot of time sailing and swimming.
We have our own sailing boat which
we like to sail in the races
in Sydney Harbour.

In Sydney the summer is warm and sunny.
We spend most of our time out of doors.
We often have a barbecue in the garden
or take a picnic down to the beach.

The hottest months of the year are
January and February.
That's when we have our long summer holidays.
We spend a lot of time on the beach then.
We once had Christmas dinner at the beach!

Most Australian children learn to swim
when they are very young.
We have a swimming pool in our back garden.
But it is more fun to go to the beach.
We often go to our nearest beach at Manly.

Sometimes we go to Bondi beach.
People like to surf there on the big waves
that roll in from the ocean.
Some stand on their surfboards and try
to balance as the waves sweep onto the beach.

Many people in Sydney like surfing.

They also play a lot of sport.

My favourite sports are tennis and cricket.

We play cricket and football at school.

On Saturdays I go to an athletics club.

One day we went on a trip with our school
to the Opera House.
This is one of the most famous buildings
in Sydney.

At the Opera House we saw a show about
the early history of Australia.
After that we went to Luna Park.
I had a ride on the big wheel.

Another school trip was to
the Royal National Park.
This is in the countryside not far
from Sydney.
We went there by coach and had a picnic
when we arrived.

The best way to see the animals in the park
is to walk silently through the bush.
If you are very lucky you might see wallabies.
Wombats and koalas also live there.

15

Wombats and koalas are not bears.
They both carry their babies in pouches.
There the babies can grow safely.
Wombats dig burrows in the ground
and eat roots.
Koalas like to sleep in the forks
of gum trees and eat the gum leaves.

Last year I went to spend the winter holidays
with my uncle.
He lives in the south of Australia.
First we went by plane to Adelaide.
It took us over four hours from Sydney.
Then we drove to his home near Port Augusta.

Much of the south and middle of Australia
is very hot and dry.
Australians call it the 'Outback'.
The biggest town in the Outback is
Alice Springs which is almost
in the middle of Australia.

Most of the roads in the Outback
don't have any fences, so wild animals
wander across them.
There are lots of kangaroos and emus here.
You can even see herds of wild camels.

The cars have 'roo' bars in front
of their engines.
These are to protect the engines and lights
if kangaroos hop into the road.
Kangaroos often get hit by cars on the roads.

Many of the cars and trucks have shields
over their windscreens.
These stop the stones which flick up
from breaking the windscreens.

Very large trucks called road trains
are used to move goods and cattle
from Alice Springs to the cities.
Road trains often travel together
across the Outback.

Children living in the Outback
don't go to school like other children.
They get their lessons through the post
once a fortnight.
They switch on a special two-way radio at home.
A teacher talks to them over the radio and
they can talk back to the teacher.

People in the Outback use the radio
to talk to each other.
They can warn each other if they need help
or say where the kangaroos
have broken down their fences.

24

They also use the radio to call up
the 'Flying Doctor' service.
The doctor talks over the radio and
says what should be done for the patient.
Sometimes the doctor flies in to take
the sick person to hospital.

My uncle has a sheep station in the Outback.
He has thousands of sheep on his station.
His stockmen work with dogs to find the sheep.
They often ride motorbikes to round them up.

When the sheep have all been rounded up,
shearers come and cut off their wool.
The men pack the wool into big bales.
They load the bales into trucks which
take the wool to be sold in the cities.

Some of the stockmen on my uncle's station
are Aborigines.
Aborigines have lived in Australia
for thousands of years.
Some of them work in the Outback and
have their own cattle stations.

Ayer's Rock near Alice Springs
belongs to the Aborigines.
The Aborigines' name for Ayer's Rock is Uluru.
The cave paintings done by Aborigines in
the caves at Uluru are very famous.

There are lots of caves at Uluru.
Long ago the Aborigines made paintings
and drawings on cave walls in many
different places in Australia.

Many of these paintings are sacred.
Others show how the Aborigines live and
how they feel about the land.
Aborigines also have many stories, dances and
songs about the animals and land in the Outback.

West of Ayer's Rock there are 28 big
rounded rocks called the Olgas.
The Olgas and Ayer's Rock can be seen
from a long way off.
Perhaps you will visit them one day.

32

Reading consultant: Diana Bentley
Editorial consultant: Donna Bailey

Illustrated by Gill Tomblin
Picture research by Suzanne Williams
Designed by Richard Garratt Design

This edition especially produced for
Macmillan Children's Books,
a division of Macmillan Publishers Limited

First published 1988

This edition published by
Macmillan Children's Books,
a division of Macmillan Publishers Limited
4 Little Essex Street, London WC2R 3LF and Basingstoke
Associated companies throughout the world

Printed in Hong Kong

British Library Cataloguing in Publication Data
Bailey, Donna
   We live in Australia.
   1. Australia. For children
   I. Title   II. Series
   994.06′3

   ISBN 0-333-47220-9

Cover: Robert Harding Picture Library
Bruce Coleman: 19 (Melinda Berge), 5 (G Bingham),
   16 (Eric Crichton), 1 (Fritz Prenzel), 18 (P R Wilkinson)
Susan Griggs Picture Agency: 23 (Ted Spiegel)
Robert Harding Picture Library: 10, 12
The Hutchison Library: 17, 21, 26, 27, 28, 30, 31
Christine Osborne: 6, 7, 8, 11, 13
Zefa: 3, 4, 20, 22, 29, 32